Pebble Plus

Animal Offspring

Ducks and Their Ducklings

by Margaret Hall

Consulting Editor: Gail Saunders-Smith, Ph.D.
Consultant: Tirath S. Sandhu, DVM, Ph.D.
Director, Cornell University Duck Research Laboratory
Eastport, New York

Capstone press

Mankato, Minnesota

Pebble Plus is published by Capstone Press
151 Good Counsel Drive, P.O. Box 669, Mankato, Minnesota 56002
http://www.capstone-press.com

1 2 3 4 5 6 08 07 06 05 04 03

Library of Congress Cataloging-in-Publication Data
Hall, Margaret, 1947–
Ducks and their ducklings/by Margaret Hall.
v. cm.—(Pebble plus: Animal offspring)
Includes bibliographical references (p. 23) and index.
Contents: Ducks—Laying eggs—Ducklings—Growing up—Watch ducks grow.
ISBN 0-7368-2106-6 (hardcover)
1. Ducklings—Juvenile literature. 2. Ducks—Juvenile literature. [1. Ducks. 2. Animals—Infancy.] I. Title. II. Series.
SF505.3 .H36 2004
636.5'97—dc21   2002155602

Editorial Credits
Sarah L. Schuette, editor; Kia Adams, series designer; Jenny Schonborn, cover production designer;
    Kelly Garvin, photo researcher; Eric Kudalis, product planning editor

Photo Credits
Bruce Coleman Inc./Scott Nielson, cover, 13; Donald White, 11
Dwight R. Kuhn, 7, 14–15, 20–21 (all)
Minden Pictures/Konrad Wothe, 4–5
PhotoDisc Inc., 18–19
Tom & Pat Leeson, 16–17
Tom Stack & Associates/Kitchin & Hurst, 1
Visuals Unlimited/Gerard Fuehrer, 8–9

Note to Parents and Teachers

The Animal Offspring series supports national science standards related to life science. This book describes and illustrates ducks and their ducklings. The images support early readers in understanding the text. The repetition of words and phrases helps early readers learn new words. This book also introduces early readers to subject-specific vocabulary words, which are defined in the Glossary section. Early readers may need assistance to read some words and to use the Table of Contents, Glossary, Read More, Internet Sites, and Index/Word List sections of the book.

Word Count: 113
Early-Intervention Level: 12

Table of Contents

Ducks

Ducks are birds with strong bills and webbed feet. Young ducks are called ducklings.

Ducks and their ducklings
live near lakes and ponds.

A female is a duck.

Sometimes a female
is called a hen.

A male is a drake.

Drakes and ducks mate.

Laying Eggs

Most ducks lay 5 to 12 eggs.

A duck sits on her eggs

to keep them warm.

Ducklings

Ducklings hatch after about one month. A duckling breaks the egg open with its egg tooth.

13

Ducklings have soft feathers called down. Ducklings will grow new feathers after two months.

Growing Up

Ducklings follow their mother to the water. She teaches them to swim and to dive.

Ducklings become adults.

Drakes and ducks fly.

Watch Ducks Grow

hatching

adult after about
four to five months

21

Glossary

bill—the hard part of a bird's mouth; ducks use their bills to peck at food; bills also are called beaks.

bird—a warm-blooded animal with wings, two legs, and feathers; birds lay eggs; most birds can fly.

egg tooth—a tooth-like part that sticks out on a duckling's bill; the egg tooth falls off shortly after the duckling hatches.

feather—one of the light, fluffy parts that covers the skin on a bird's body; ducks have waterproof feathers.

hatch—to break out of an egg; ducklings hatch from their eggs after about one month.

mate—to join together to produce young

webbed—having folded skin or tissue between an animal's toes or fingers; ducks have webbed feet to help them swim better.

Read More

Gibbons, Gail. *Ducks!* New York: Holiday House, 2001.

Goldin, Augusta R. *Ducks Don't Get Wet.* Let's Read and Find Out Science. New York: HarperCollinsPublishers, 1999.

Hipp, Andrew. *The Life Cycle of a Duck.* The Life Cycles Library. New York: PowerKids Press, 2002.

Morgan, Sally. *How Things Grow from Egg to Duck.* How Things Grow. North Mankato, Minn.: Thameside Press, 2002.

Internet Sites

Do you want to find out more about ducks and their ducklings? Let FactHound, our fact-finding hound dog, do the research for you.

Here's how:

1) Visit *http://www.facthound.com*

2) Type in the **Book ID** number: 0736821066

3) Click on **FETCH IT**.

FactHound will fetch Internet sites picked by our editors just for you!

Index/Word List